THE SECRET OF BARBERING

A SCIENCE

—FOR—

PRACTICAL USE IN BARBERING.

By R. W. BOOKER

Dedicated to My Deceased Mother,
MRS. ANN AMELIA BOOKER.

Preface.

IN order to meet the enormous public demand and one which becomes more and more pressing, to have published a thorough scientific treatise on the art of barbering, this book has been issued. We have endeavored to supply this great demand by a work containing several photographic casts illustrating all the various positions needed in honing, stropping, shaving and hair cutting. The following points of information are those which the author has wrought out through a long life of tedious, though successful practice and hard study. The author, as a thoroughly accomplished manipulator in every phase of barbering, fearlessly offers this work to the shrewdest criticism of the most efficient barbers in the land. He also guarantees that the barber apprentice will find its efficiency boundless; a work in which all the finer parts of the trade are treated in detail.

Yet the reading matter is plain, simple, comprehensive, concise, to the point and exhaustive. It is further guaranteed the apprentice that by procuring a copy of this work, he will be able to acquire his trade at a cost incomparably small, both in time and money, and be benefited in an inestimably greater degree than he could possibly otherwise be.

The student of "THE SECRET OF BARBERING" will always have an authentic reference near at hand for consultation until he becomes thoroughly proficient; whereas, on the other hand, the apprentice without the aid of "THE SECRET OF BARBERING" is obliged to depend upon his ever-fading memory; and to learn his trade after all by his own efforts, struggling through a long series of unpardonable blunders. Trusting that this work will be of service to my countrymen, I remain,

Respectfully yours,

BENJAMIN WOODSON BOOKER.

DESCRIPTION OF THE RAZOR

THE HAIR

USE NO WATER on the hair except when really necessary, which is only when one is undergoing the process of shampooing, or when cutting a pompadour. Water will utterly ruin most heads of hair, by removing the oil secreted by the oil glands, thus destroying the natural gloss, and leaving the hair rough, refractory and unattractive. Moreover, for the same reason it causes the hair to fall out.

There is only the motive of vanity to impel one to use water on the hair. Therefore my admonition is to comb the hair dry, training it the way it should go by frequent combing and brushing.

GOOD WORK

We admit that many a man is doing fairly good work in barbering, but a better knowledge of the various parts of barbering, would qualify him to do most excellent work. There are plenty of average men engaged in the tonsorial profession, as in all other kinds of business, but what is most needed are the excellent workmen.

Give barbering your undivided attention until you master it. Not until then would it be advisable to study on any other line of thought. It would be a great detriment to your own interest in reaching the highest attainment in barbering. One is not so apt to cut a subject when shaving if razors are kept sharp. When in good condition they cut the beard well; when dull they are likely to cut the face.

Use your best razors at all times, on all classes of trade, and have none other than good ones; it pays in the end, at the beginning and all along. It is the best way to advertise. Good tools, in good condition, well manipulated, are incentives to work of the highest class, which stands alone, and wins out over all other forms of barbering.

PREPARATORY WORK

THOSE who start out to acquire a knowledge of the art of barbering, should first have a preparatory course before entering into the real work of barbering. The preparatory part of the work comes in the form of shaving necks, combing and dressing the hair, lathering and bathing faces and necks, and stropping and honing razors. The last two named require a great deal of practice.

STROPPING AND HONING

IN STROPPING, use an old razor that can not be utilized for shaving purposes, because a good razor would soon become worthless, as the result of too much heat produced by friction from constant passing of the blade over the strop for the time necessary for one's practice. This exercise in stropping should be kept up at intervals until such skill is attained that in turning the razor it may be passed over the strop with great velocity, without injuring the strop by cutting it. Then when turning to the real work you may be able to apply the razor to the strop accurately and decisively. It is well for me to state here the object of stropping. The object of stropping is to get the benefit of the temper the blade contains, the greater portion of which is stored up in the thickest part of the blade, technically termed the back of the razor. Hence stropping becomes necessary in order to draw it down to the edge, which is done by the friction caused by stropping. Then, when razors are laid aside in the best possible condition, and allowed to remain for any reasonable time, they will not cut well until they are stropped again, for the simple reason that the temper travels back to the thickest part of the blade and leaves the thin edge comparatively without temper. Therefore the razor should not be held too flat on the strop but tipped at an angle of about ten degrees in order to concentrate the temper right along the edge of the blade. This is the most essential point in stropping, that of holding the razor obliquely upon the strop [See Fig. 1], turn it upon its back, stropping both sides alike [See Figs. 1 & 2] which represent the two strokes necessary in stropping. The first stroke [See Fig. 1], drawing the razor towards you upon the strop, the back of the razor towards you. No. 2 represents the second stroke sending it from you, the back of the razor from you always turning it upon its back.

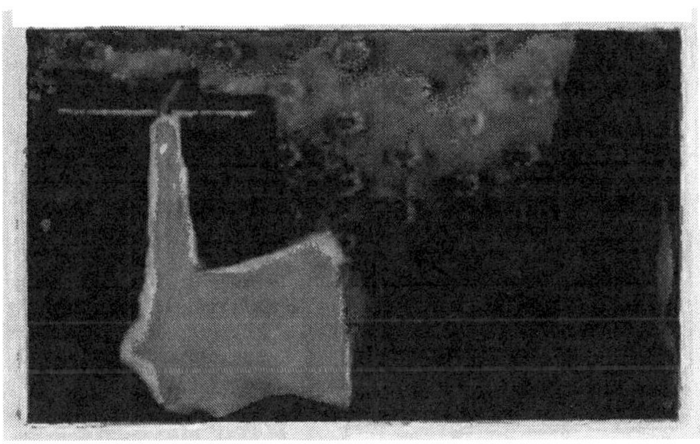

Fig. 3

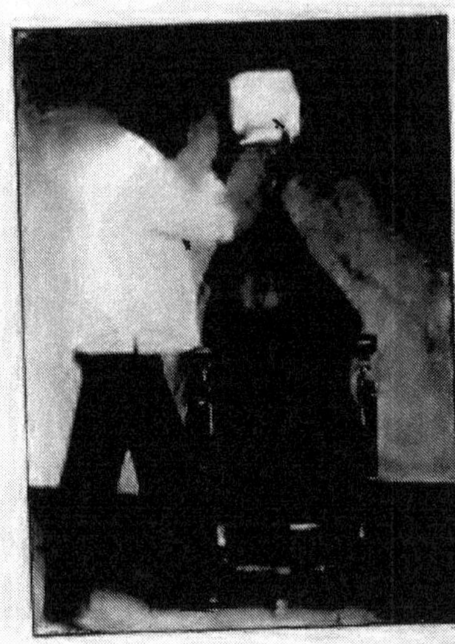

Fig. 4

HONING

FOR THIS line of the work, a special training is needed also, preparatory to mastering the art of honing. The exercises in honing, must be practiced at intervals, with an old razor, in order to become proficient in the manipulation of the blade upon the hone, both to and fro, edge to and edge from, as is required in the actual practice of honing. This practice should be kept up until one is familiar with the movements so very necessary in sharpening razors. When this has been accomplished, the tools that are to be employed in actual service may be ventured upon. To hone razors well, the hone must never be held in the hand or upon anything that is unsteady, but must be upon something solid, that will not give a particle, so as to put an edge upon the blade evenly. In turning the razor upon the hone, turn it upon its back. Always apply it evenly to the hone, both sides of the razor, to and fro, holding it flat on the hone, but do not draw it squarely towards you but in a position represented by Fig. 3, Fig. 4 representing the stroke from you. Now in beginning to hone a razor, first discover what it needs. Possibly it may have nicks in the edge. Ordinary honing would not do in this case, but the nicks must first be taken out. They are not always visible to the naked eye; so the safest way to be sure about these little but important matters, is, to moisten the thumb or finger nail by touching it to your tongue and drawing the edge of the razor across the moistened nail. If there are any defects in the blade, you will certainly find them by resorting to this method. A great many barbers use the end of the finger to test a razor, even to tell when it is sharp, but that is a very unsatisfactory way as the end of the finger is not solid enough. When the razor passes over it, it gives way too much for one to ascertain the difficulty. Therefore I advise you to use the thumb or finger nail in order to discover these defects. These nicks are taken out by standing the razor almost perpendicularly upon the hone and operating it in that position. Just where the nicks are should be the only part of the razor to come in contact with the hone. In this way the nicks are removed in much less time than by the old way of laying the blade flat upon the hone, and honing an hour or more.

Now, as to honing razors for service, Figs. 3 and 4 represent the two important positions in honing, when the hone rests upon a table, bench or whatever may be used. Figure 3 represents the first stroke towards you. The razor has been turned upon its back, and Fig. 4 now represents the second stroke in honing. This is to be kept up until the razor is perfectly sharp. From the beginning of this exercise, moisten the thumb or finger nail frequently and draw the edge of the razor across it lightly. At first it may seem rough. but as you go farther on with the intelligence that Figs. 3 and 4 afford, you will notice that the edge is becoming smoother and that it begins to adhere to the moistened finger nail. Carry it all the way from the heel to the point, over the nail, and you will observe the edge as it is coming on and can tell what part of the blade needs the most honing. As this process is kept up, the blade sticks the tighter to the nail, which is firm enough to tell you when the edge is sharp, or nicked or rough. So, when the razor adheres from heel to point, it is in very fine condition, and is technically called a "well honed razor." In Fig. 3, the edge is drawn towards you, in Fig. 4 the edge goes from you. In this position unusual care should be used as it is not as handy to apply the razor to the hone in this stroke as in the stroke that applies it to the hone in Fig. 3, consequently the stroke shown in Fig. 4, often goes its route without cutting away a particle of the material of the side of the razor for which this stroke is intended, and but one side is honed and the razor is condemned, when the fault is in the operator and not in the implement. This is the case; actual honing and actual stropping are the essential features and are really indispensible in good shaving.

Then when is a razor honed? When it sticks closely to the moistened finger nail. How then do you strop a razor? By tipping it a little occasionally when using the strop. [See Fig. 1]. This figure represents the stroke towards you in which case the blade is held in an oblique position upon the strop, no part touching the strop but the edge itself.

STROPPING

NOW, after razors are honed, the next thing is the stropping. The strops used are usually three in number, the canvas and two other finer or finishing strops. The canvas is the first to be used and a very brisk stropping should be given to all freshly honed razors, upon this strop. Fig. 2 represents the brisk forward stroke, utilizing the whole strop in this stroke. The back of the blade is sent from and is just the reverse of the stroke represented by Fig. 1. In stropping, the razor is manipulated to the reverse of its position in honing; the back of the blade, comes to and the back goes from; in honing the edge of the blade comes to and the edge goes from. Strops should always be kept in good order. Canvas strops should be loaded with beeswax. Take a ball of beeswax and rub it thoroughly upon this strop, filling its pores and polishing off with the

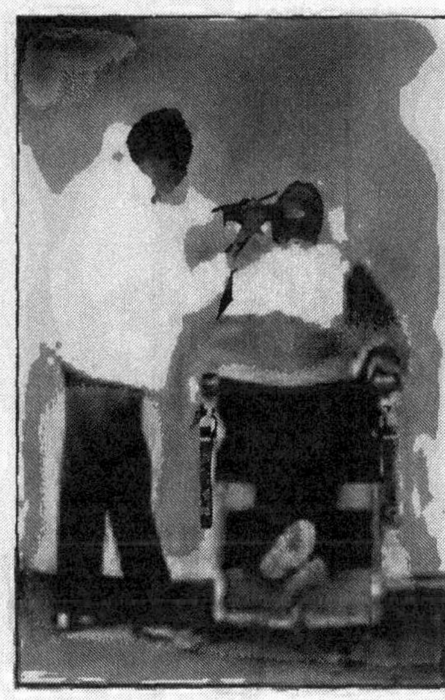

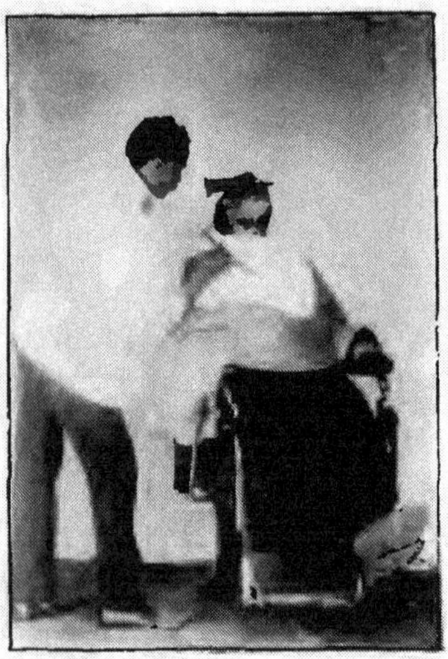

Fig 7

Fig. 8

SHAVING

NOW, having our strops and razors in good order, I call your attention to the real work, the Shaving of the man in the chair. Lather the face first and rub it into the beard thoroughly; then, with warm water, wash the beard, thus softening the hair and getting it into good condition; then lather the second time, and the Shaving begins. Herein is the "secret of barbering." Attention is called to the nine figures, 5 to 13 inclusive which represent the first nine important positions in Shaving the first time over. In these nine positions, the black upon the subject's face represents the lather so it may be plainly seen just how far the barber may shave in that position in which he is working without doing injury to the subject's face. Fig. 5 shows where the lather has been shaved off; the face is bare as in any ordinary case of shaving. To shave farther than this cut shows, in the position in which the barber is standing, would not be wise, so in order to further the cause in Shaving, Fig. 6 shows the next position really necessary. Here is one that should teach a great lesson, both in shaving and in the manner the razor is held in the hand. The stroke in this cut is backhanded.

I will say for your convenience here, that almost all the movements in Shaving, are wris movements, and not whole arm movements; so in this backhanded shaving, let the arm be as steady as possible, but let the wrist move with unusual velocity, and practice no long strokes, but ordinary ones. In long stroke shaving the razor is fed too fast, and cannot cut well. In cases where razors do, they are rare ones. In the case which Fig. 6 represents you will notice that the barber has shaved around to the middle of the chin. This is very essential, for if it be not shaved fully half way, when coming around from the opposite side, as is shown in figure 10, one would be very apt to cut the subject's face. Here is where the work must meet evenly from both sides of the face. Any other way would fail to accomplish the desired result. Shave with the grain, or the way the beard grows, as much as possible. This is the best way for shaving the first time off; but after that for close shaving, shave against and across the grain as the case suggests itself for the safety and comfort of the patron.

Fig. 7 shows just how far down on the neck one should shave and no farther; for in ninety-nine cases out of one hundred, the beard runs down only just so far as is shown in Fig. 7. Shaving down as is shown is necessary, for it is best to shave with the beard or with the grain the first time over. Fig. 8 is the fourth position. It is the safest and best It calls for more time in stepping around the chair than any other in executing this part of the work, that of shaving up with the beard as it grows on the neck. In reference to the third position, should one shave all the way down the neck, the result would be a very sore neck, badly broken out and covered with pimples. So it becomes necessary to resort to the aid of the fourth position. Although many barbers have adopted the overhand, upward stroke as is shown in Fig. 17, fourth position in close shaving, in order to save the time it requires to step around the chair, but it is not a safe thing to do. This position, Fig. 17, is only a relative position in close shaving. Fig. 9 requires the face to be turned toward you and the backhanded forward movement continued, an exact repetition of the holding of the razor as is seen in Fig. 6, and shows just how far one can execute the work while remaining in

Fig. 9

Fig 10

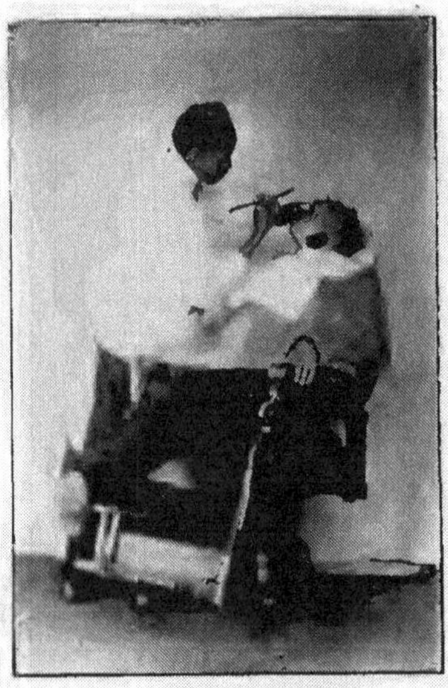

Fig 11

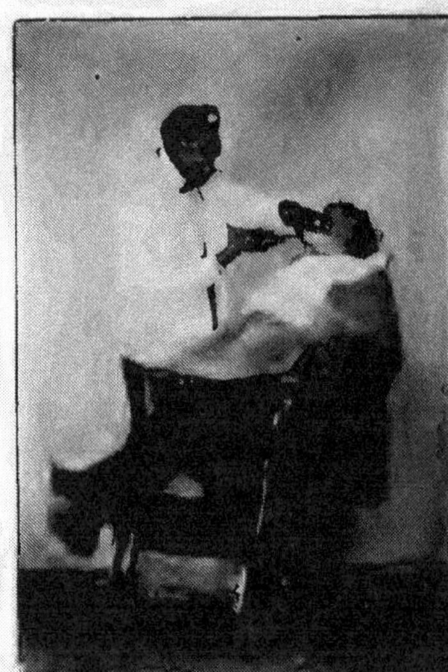

Fig 12

position 5. The black which represents the lather upon the face of the subject continues to diminish and outlines the work in the manner in which all shaving as a profession should be done. So you may observe from Fig. 10, that the work has been extended to the chin of the subject and is united with the work already executed in the first four positions, omitting the 9th. Observe, during the process of shaving, in all the various positions how the razor is held in the hand. It is necessary to know this and highly necessary to practice it until it is perfected, if barbering is to be your avocation.

Fig. 11 shows just how far to shave down on the neck. It is the same intent as Fig. 7, only on the opposite side of the face and backhanded shaving just as far as the beard grows down the neck. Fig. 12 dispenses with the lather save what little remains upon the upper lip as is shown in Fig. 13. Fig. 12 represents shaving upwards on the neck. This includes the first nine important positions in shaving the first time over. Fig. 10 has, in some instances, a minor position in uniting the work of the two sides of the face at the chin in shaving the first time over. That position is when the work has been united at the chin. Underneath it should be shaved by whatever position you may desire or by raising the chin of the subject and using the heel of the razor generally. Fig. 13 represents shaving the upper lip, backhanded strokes.

These nine positions will remove the beard of any one who has to be shaved and in many cases are perfectly satisfactory to him who wants to be shaved only once over, but does not answer for all, so, having given the facts upon the subject of shaving for the first time over, we shall call attention to our next which includes close shaving.

CLOSE SHAVING

Fifteen of the best and most important positions in close shaving are here described. Immediately after the subject has been shaved over the first time, rinse the face well with water in order to clear away all the soap from the face, so that it may not smart when the second operation in close shaving begins.

In case of close shaving, have a piece of alum in the hand, moisten the hand and take hold of the alum. This prevents the hands slipping. Lose as little time as possible after rinsing the face, for the beard soon dries and becomes hard again.

In order to avoid this, Fig. 14 shows the barber at work upon the side of the face that was first shaved. This is a very important position. Shave while the beard is soft, always carrying as much water as possible on the face during the entire process of close shaving, or after the lather has been washed off. This water keeps the razor from burning the face and causing it to smart, as, in some cases, happens even when the shaving was done in some of the best shops and by some of the best artists in the land. Often times barbers set a man's face on fire, comparatively speaking by lathering one side and shaving it and leaving the other side bare, then lathering the bare side and immediately shaving it. In no case of this kind can one make time in shaving or give comfort to your patron, for beards cannot, as a general rule, be put in condition in so little time as this process of shaving requires, so it is best at all times to lather the whole face, unless one calls for a dry shave

Fig. 13

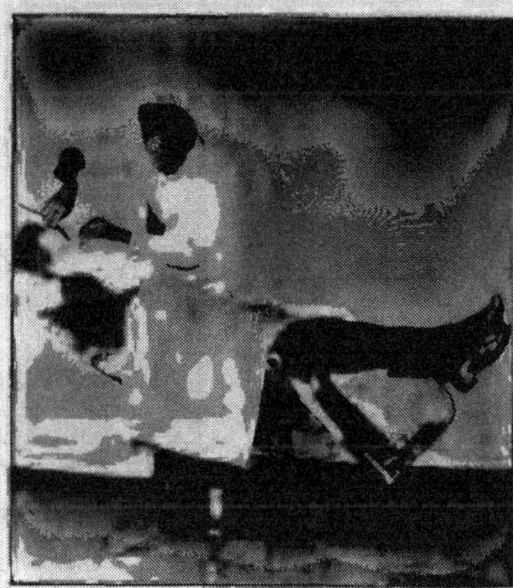

Fig. 14

Fig 15

Fig 16

which is done by softening the beard with warm water and not using any lather at all, continuing to use warm water through the whole process.

While shaving let the razor blade lie almost flat on the face. It cuts much better, for in most cases or with a great many barbers, the razor stands up at much too great an angle, possibly fifteen degrees. It seems reasonable to say that in such a position it is scraping and not shaving.

Fig. 15 is a relative position to Fig. 14, tightening the skin of the face as you will observe from left hand of barber at work in this position, tightening the skin of the face being very essential in all forms of shaving and one should not become neglectful in this.

WATER IN SHAVING

One important practice—always use as great an amount of water as it is possible to use comfortably. In Fig. 15 the barber is shaving upward under the chin and on the neck and in cases where beards grow round in a circle under the chin as beards often do, a form of shaving called "rolling the flesh" as seen in Fig. 20 is the best to adopt when working in position 15 or any other position in which it may be adopted. By this way of shaving, the subject can be treated without injury.

Fig. 16 illustrates shaving nearest side of face with backhanded strokes and wrist movement, arm steady. Fig. 17 is a relative position used often in shaving the first time over doing same work as Fig. 8. The position of the left hand, Fig. 18 shows spreading the face, with the forward stroke of the razor which is held in a slanting position. This slanting position which covers all styles of shaving, can be used to advantage more frequently than any other position in the entire work. The spreading of the skin and the slanting of the razor when in service are two very important factors in the execution of good shaving Fig. 19 is used only in close shaving and is an overhand, ambidexterous stroke and is the only stroke that can successfully take away all the beard from along the jawbone of the face, which gives comfort to so many who desire close shaving. This ambidexterous stroke is the one in which the whole arm movement is brought into play, and should be practiced a great deal as it is very difficult to master, but can be mastered and will become as easy as any other stroke in barbering. In this position one may plainly see how the razor is to be held in the hand when shaving, the handle passing between the little finger and the one next to it and between the thumb and forefinger. This is the correct way. Again it may be seen in Fig. 17. Note the facts for they are of untold value to him who follows barbering as an avocation. One may become weary of the many positions I give in high class barbering, and the talk that becomes necessary to unfold to you the Secret of Barbering; but nevertheless that does not detract anything from the value of this work. So I shall continue with the remaining nine positions, the first of which is Fig. 20. This figure is used in very close shaving and is called "rolling the flesh." In this manner of manipulating the face, the beard is forced out from its cells and can be cut off without pain, as close as is possible to have it cut, and when plenty of water is used, faces are kept in good condition and the work is generally satisfactory. Some faces will not stand this method of close shaving. You may know this by the ap-

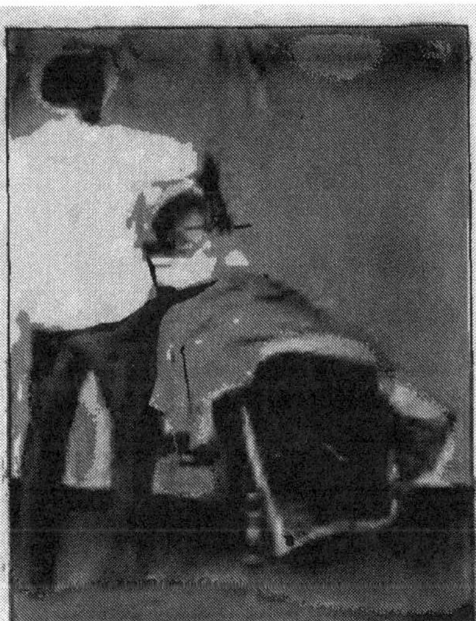

Fig 17

Fig 18

Fig. 19

pearance of little red blotches, or white pimples a day or so after shaving. The following two Figs. 21 and 22 come under the head of very close shaving. This process is called "kneading the face." In Fig. 21 in very close shaving the skin is drawn out and over the four fingers which are underneath the folds of the skin and out of view. These four fingers are pushing the skin up and crowding out the beard, and the thumb, all of which may be seen, is drawing the upper surface to a level so that the razor may pass over and do the work for which this position calls. A great many men can never feel comfortable after shaving because they can, when shaved feel beard along under the neck as Fig. 21 shows and is above mentioned. Fig. 21 is "kneading the face;" so is Fig. 22. There cannot be a vestige of beard left upon the face or neck when one resorts to the method of close shaving as represented by Fig. 22, a form of kneading the face that stands by itself alone in this case as represented by Fig. 22. The thumb and forefinger spread the face or neck and the three fingers are underneath as the skin is drawn, working the beard out that is too deep seated to be caught any other way.

Fig. 23 is the position in shaving the upper lip, drawing the razor toward you, Fig. 24, shaving the lip also with backhanded strokes, shaving from. Fig. 25 in very close shaving shows that but very little of the razor blade can be seen for the reason that the thumb has been moved down the blade almost to the end of it. No one knows but those who follow this style of shaving, the comfort it gives to the subject being shaved and with what grace and ease the beards can be amputated by holding the razor in this manner. This manner of holding the razor is highly recommended and can be adopted in many a position in shaving. All work in close shaving is usually against the grain or across it. This system of close shaving is useful to persons who have shaved for many years, rather than beneficial to younger men, and persons who know not the results from years of steady shaving. In rare cases and generally with elderly men, close shaving may be carried down on the neck, shaving also against the grain or against the beard or across the beard until the neck is perfectly clean of any beard at all, without doing harm but not often is this the case.

Fig. 26, in close shaving, illustrates pinching up the face. Tightening, another form of kneading the face, is useful and should be practiced. Fig. 27 illustrates kneading the face. This is not along the jawbone but under the neck, where men who shave close like to have this part of the work done well. The thumb is underneath in this case, pushing the beard out of the cells, while the razor passes over it and severs it so deeply that when the skin is relaxed there can not be left a particle of beard. Fig. 28 completes the work. Here the barber shaves downward and not a vestige of beard remains. These fifteen positions include what is called "rolling the flesh" and "kneading the face," both of which give comfort to your patrons and are soothing and refreshing. These fifteen positions are indeed the most beautiful ones in shaving, to him who has patience to work them out. There should be plenty of time allowed in which to shave one, unless a quick shave is desired by the patron, or some other cause prevents the barber from tarrying long with his customer. Plenty of time in most cases gives comfort, and general satisfaction to the patrons. Therefore it endears them to your place of business; whereas a great many leave a shop never to return because of so little time given in shaving.

Having said enough along the line of shaving, and knowing that what facts the Secret of Bar-

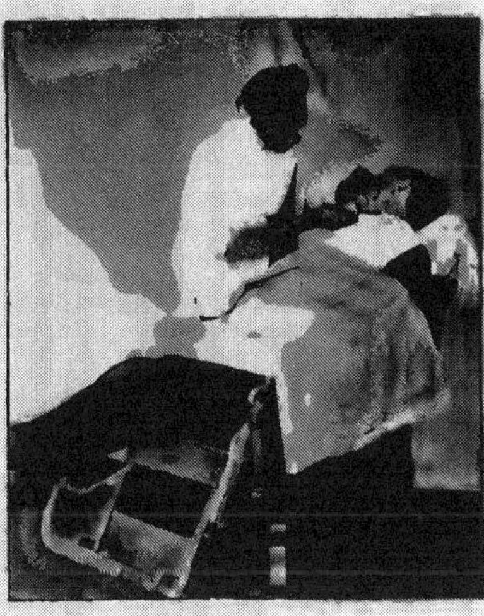

Fig 20

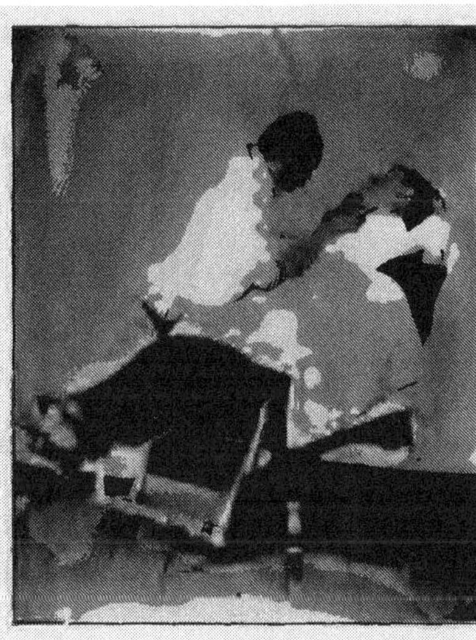

Fig. 21

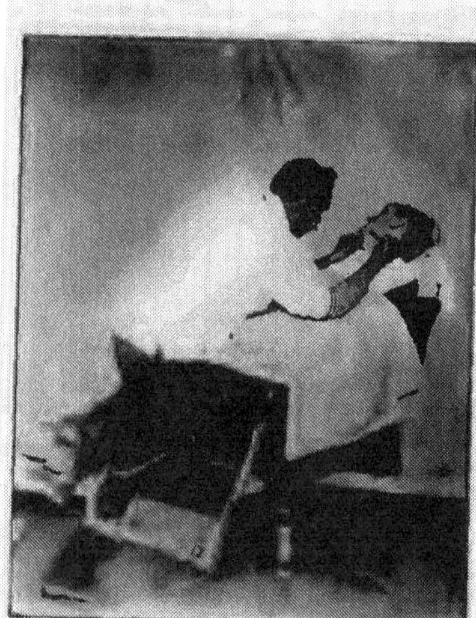

Fig. 22

Fig. 23

bering fails to give, your own practical experience will impart, as these already given are the most important, we therefore conclude shaving and call attention to hair cutting.

HAIR CUTTING

THE first style is represented by Fig. 29. This and the remaining three figures—30 31 and 32—are high class society work, and known as swell-hair cutting. The designs for swell hair cutting run as follows: Quarter moon, half moon and full moon, all of which represent the moon's phases.

Fig. 29 represents a quarter moon in temple work as a swell finish in high class barbering and is very beautiful and much preferred by many to any other style in swell hair cutting. This cut extends only half way around the temple, or about half as far as 30's work shows. Fig. 30 represents a half moon in temple work as a swell finish in high class barbering and is very much to be admired as it is becoming in many cases, and most especially for persons who have full growth over the temples, but can not be used in all cases of hair cutting because, as before intimated, all temples have not a full enough growth of hair for the line of survey which this half moon is designed to show. Square-cut temple work and pointed temple work, or any other style of temple finish one may adopt, does not belong in the category of swell hair-cutting and are not rated as high class society work, but decidedly inferior to it. Therefore, Figs. 29 and 30 are the most important of all the designs in temple work. Fig. 31 shows a full moon cut and is paramount to all other styles of cutting the hair, and can be used to a great advantage in any style of hair cutting, and should be generally adopted. In the case of a good full moon the hair is combed down over the forehead and cut off as much on one side as the other. The line of survey should begin, say at the left high temple, as the cut shows, and extend down in a circle to the eyes and across and upon the right high temple in just as even proportions as is possible for it to be. Then let the hair be combed out often and ends cut where irregular in order that this work, the full moon, may be true, neither side left longer than the other. In this way the hair never bothers one by getting down in his eyes and can be parted in the middle or on either side with the best possible results. In these styles of hair cutting I deem it wise to mention this fact, that the hair must be allowed to grow out full all over the head, then when cutting the hair you may give the head the desired shape as shown in Fig. 32. This is a puff cut, full moon, back and front, quarter moon, temples. You may be able to satisfy in a reasonable measure your trade with mechanical hair cutting and with mechanical shaving, but they will be much better satisfied with artistic hair cutting and artistic shaving. Therefore, be it remembered that in these styles of swell hair cutting, the hair must not be cut off too high up the back of the head, as the head then loses its shape, but must be left long so as to come entirely down over the mole of the head, the work all being done at the base of the head, and around the sides, never cutting the hair close enough for the scalp to show through, for where the scalp is shown that kind of work comes under the head of "tight hair cutting." Then we readily discover that we have two systems of hair cutting, namely "tight" hair cutting, and "long" hair cutting, of which the designs in swell society work as represented by cuts or Figs. 29, 30, 31, 32 govern them all. For Fig. 32 there are other designs for finishing the neck which are not herein illustrated. They are mentioned, as styles for finishing the neck, in the following order, "round," which means a full moon, as you see in Fig. 32, "long branch," which is shaving down the sides of the neck, and "square," which is shaping the neck squarely across. The clippers are usually used on the neck in the case of shaping the neck "long branch" style, in order that the line of survey on either side should be brought out evenly and without ragged edges. And in all cases of shaping the neck and temples let the line of survey extend far enough into the hair, so that the desired effect may be perfectly clear, for which this line is most available.

Fig. 33 and the following Figs. 34, 35 and 36 are representing work of a high order in pompadour hair cutting, which in this case is "tight" hair cutting. The clippers, of what ever length may be desired, are used on the back and sides of the head, as may be seen in Fig. 35, far up on the temples as all clipper work should be done, in order that the work may be systematic and also corresponding with the tightness of the clippers which the head will show, the clippers being the first step taken in this style of hair cutting; the next is Fig. 33: the hair should be combed out thoroughly and cut off in the shape of a full moon as seen on Fig. 31. Cut far up, almost to the edge of the scalp. Notice the line drawn across the forehead of Fig. 33. All the hair cut away would leave the forehead bare, its appearance then would be unbecoming, but next moisten the hair that remains so as it may stand up well, and then take position behind the chair as seen in Fig. 35, and after having combed it all up, begin where the clippers left off and work forward with the comb, always combing toward you. Cut the hair down about the length you desire the pompadour and comb it down again, and move forward to the front and begin to comb up again, at the same time shingle off the front, which, when done just right, makes a beautiful oval shaped pompadour cut, as seen in Fig. 35. Not square at all, but oval in shape, which is proper. Then by joining the clipper work and that of the shears, as is shown by Fig 35, in this case the barber is joining the work together, a very tedious task and one that requires a great deal of attention before the work is made smooth.

Fig. 36 shows the barber taking observations of the way the hair lies; in looking this way the slightest defect can be plainly seen and taken out. Fig. 34, the barber combs and brushes up the pompadour, and his work is finished, as the workmanship is oval in shape and uniform in style and is the only shape for up-to-date pompadour hair cutting, as shown in Fig. 34.

TIGHT HAIR CUTTING.

The Secret of Barbering will now introduce to you its last style of hair cutting which comes under the form of "tight" hair cutting and is known as a "crown cut." This style is very suitable for boys, mill men, factory men, coal miners, railroad men or those engaged in any work in which the head gets dirty very quickly. With this cut the head can be kept clean with much less effort than with any other style excepting the pompadour.

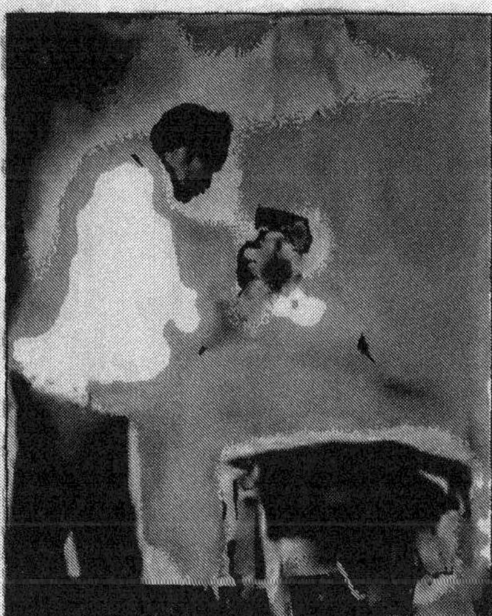

Fig. 24

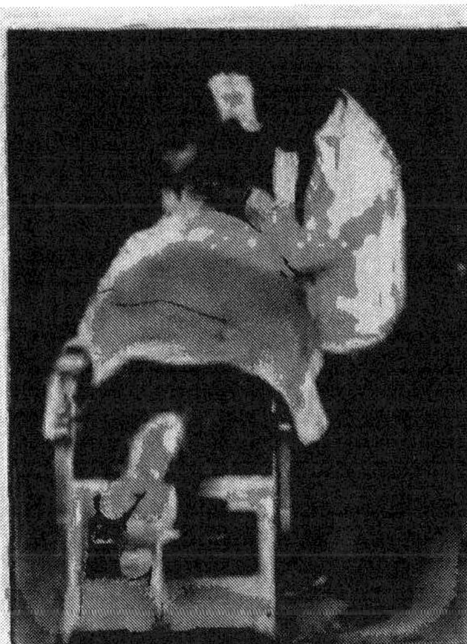

Fig 25

Fig. 26

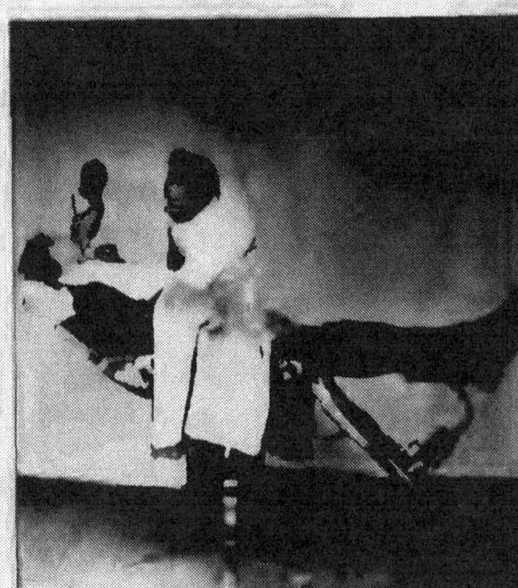

Fig. 27

Fig. 28

Fig. 29

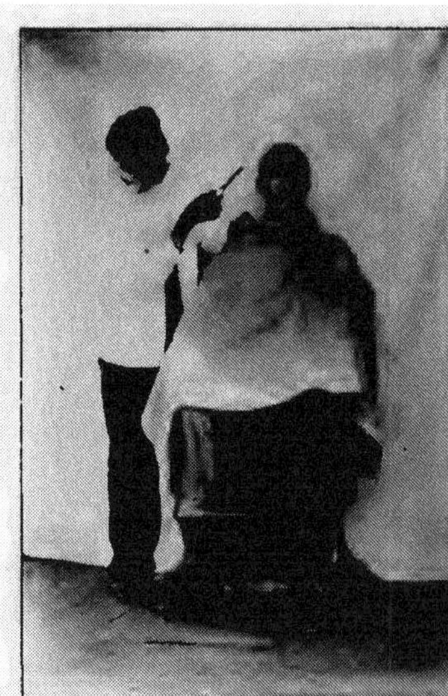

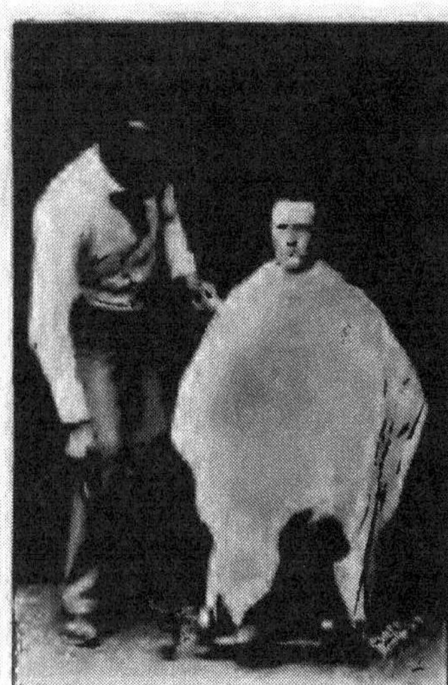

Fig. 34

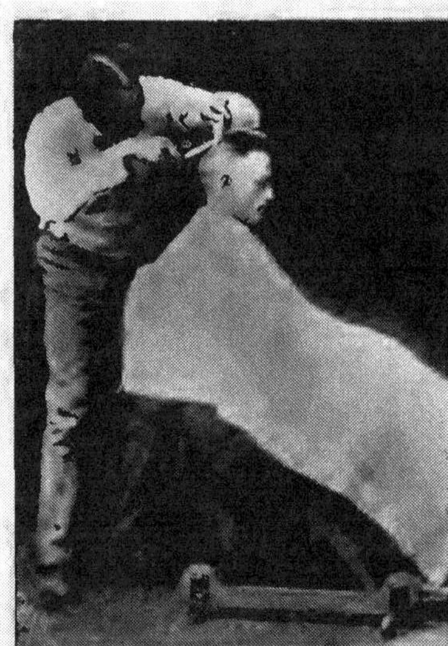

Fig. 35

Fig. 37 and Fig. 38 show the work as it is being executed in crown hair cutting. Fig. 37 shows the foretop for boys, the design is a full moon. In this cut you may notice that the hair is cut shorter for boys than for men; for boys the full moon comes about half way down the forehead, for men it should come down to the eyes, or near it, as shown in Fig. 31. Fig. 38 shows that the particular and all important feature in "tight" hair cutting is being executed, that of joining together perfectly the work of the clippers and that of the shears.

MISCELLANEOUS BARBERING.

Avoid using rotten soaps on faces. The cause of soaps softening in the mug, or rotting, is that the general way of many workmen is to place a new cake of soap on top of one nearly used up in the mug. This lets the water in under the whole business and it will decay in a few days—if shop is kept warm, will sour. This should not be done but remnants of cake of soap should be taken ou of mug and mug washed and dried, and the new cake beaten out, if too small, so as to fit the mug and placed in perfectly dry and the remnant on the top of it. All the soap is used then, none wasted and always in good condition.

Clean towels, clean shop and clean self and pleasing attitude are criticisms that should govern if success is anticipated.

When trimming beards almost any style clippers can be used on the neck in order to maket a neat job.

CURLING THE MUSTACHE.

The best way is to use tissue paper and roll the mustache around it just as you would wrap a string around a match. When tight enough plait the end of the paper and let it stand awhile, if crimpers are preferred don't have them too hot, that breaks the hairs off.

Shampooing the head once every week or oftener, has a great tendency to increase dandruff, therefore abstain from so much shampooing. It takes away too much of the natural oil of the hair. In cases where it becomes necessary to shampoo very often quite a deal of oil or vasaline should be used afterwards. Egg shampooing is the best. Break whole egg into a cup or small bowl; to this add a small amount of bay rum, a little witch-hazel and Florida water; to this add enough shampoo so as to make a good lather and beat all together. Beat it well, then saturate the hair and scalp, thoroughly rubbing the head with a rough brush used for that purpose, then rinse. A dry shampoo is one given in the chair without putting the customer's head under the water spout. Rinse the head well with towels until all is clean, just as he sits in the barber chair. There are many who do not like the water spout.

Razors should not have thorough honing oftener than once a week; if they do not hold up well have the hone handy and in a moment's time, to and fro across the hone, the edge will come on perfectly. After the face is lathered, in this way the edge can be put properly on the razor before the lather dries, and by touching it up as aforesaid one razor may be made to execute for one whole week the heaviest work appertaining to barbering.

Fig. 36

Fig. 37

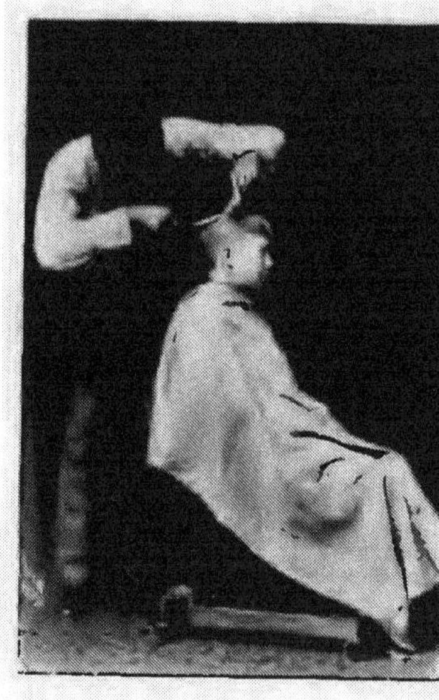

Fig 38

When stropping in this oblique position of the razor upon the strop, care should be used or the razor may be held too perpendicular. Strokes in this manner would round the edge and prevent its use at all.

When shaving practice as light a hand as possible, never holding a firm grip upon the razor —this is a detriment. Barely hold it and no more.

Arguments should not be indulged in, and when they arise in the shop decide with the customer as often as possible, even if he be wrong.

When softening the beards for shaving rub the lather into them briskly but do not bear too hard upon the face, as this will largely dispense with the comfort that belongs with good shaving.

Razors that are good should have rest occasionally, this enhances their longevity.

Do not accept pay for your labor and then refuse to compensate others for their services.

When cutting hair, it should be cut so evenly all over the entire head, that no defects can be seen at all. Usually every stroke of the shears can be seen in the hair that is cut after the manner of some workmen, which shows the inability of that workman to execute first class work. Be true workmen. The most excellent workmen are the most needed.

CONCLUSION.

Having given you the facts in hair cutting, shaving, honing and stropping, as they came to me during fifteen years of ardent study and from practical experience, my oblations I now render you through the columns of this little book. The Secret of Barbering will conclude with the following advice:

Who loves his trade with all his heart
  Has learned one secret of the art,
The Key is here in black and white—
  The Key that opes the door to light,
The Key that turns the lock of fame:
  On her fair tablet write your name.

Your well wisher,

B. W. BOOKER.

CPSIA information can be obtained
at www.ICGtesting.com
Printed in the USA
LVHW022055310323
743149LV00011B/1176

9 780343 940867